GLOBAL PRODUCTS

GPS

G. S. PRENTZAS

Published in the United States of America
by Cherry Lake Publishing, Ann Arbor, Michigan
www.cherrylakepublishing.com

Content Adviser
Colin Brooks, Research Scientist, Michigan Tech Research Institute

Credits
Photos: Cover and page 1, ©knotsmaster, used under license from Shutterstock, Inc.; page 4, ©iStockphoto.com/KingWu; page 6, ©artpartner-images.com/Alamy; page 9, ©Lorraine Kourafas, used under license from Shutterstock, Inc.; page 10, ©iStockphoto.com/robas; page 12, ©iStockphoto.com/mabus13; page 14, ©michael ledray, used under license from Shutterstock, Inc.; page 17, ©Yury Kosourov, used under license from Shutterstock, Inc.; page 18, ©Fleyeing/Dreamstime.com; page 20, ©AP Photo/Reed Hoffmann; page 22, ©Kai-Uwe Och/Alamy; page 24, ©p_a_p_a, used under license from Shutterstock, Inc.; page 26, ©AP Photo/Douglas C. Pizac

Map by XNR Productions Inc.

Library of Congress Cataloging-in-Publication Data
Prentzas, G. S.
GPS / by G.S. Prentzas.
p. cm.—(Global products)
Includes bibliographical references and index.
ISBN-13: 978-1-60279-506-8
ISBN-10: 1-60279-506-1
1. GPS receivers—Juvenile literature. 2. Manufacturing processes—Juvenile literature. 3. Globalization—Juvenile literature. I. Title. II. Series.
TK6565.D5P74 2009
910.285—dc22 2008053633

Cherry Lake Publishing would like to acknowledge
the work of The Partnership for 21st Century Skills.
Please visit *www.21stcenturyskills.org* for more information.

TABLE OF CONTENTS

GPS

CHAPTER ONE

PERSONAL NAVIGATION

Brandon and his friend Tommy piled into the backseat of the minivan. "Mom," said Brandon, "here's the invitation." Mrs. Allen was driving the two teenagers to a birthday party for their classmate Leela. Mrs. Allen used a

GPS units are popular with people who spend a lot of time driving.

touch screen to enter Leela's address into a GPS unit attached to the dashboard. The screen displayed a map with local streets and the minivan's location. "*Turn left onto Prospect Drive and proceed for 0.3 mile,*" a female voice from the unit advised.

Tommy peered over the front seat. "Hey, my dad wants one of those!" he exclaimed.

Mrs. Allen replied, "They're great for getting somewhere without getting lost. The unit receives information from **satellites** in the sky and calculates where you are. When you enter an address, the unit's computer figures out the best route to get there."

Tommy wondered aloud, "How does it do that?"

Mrs. Allen responded, "I'm not exactly sure. Let's ask Leela's mother. She teaches science at the university. I'm sure she'll know."

"*You have arrived at your destination.*"

Leela's mother answered the door and welcomed the boys to the party. "Hi, I'm Seeta Bose," she said to Mrs. Allen. "It's nice to finally meet you."

Mrs. Allen replied, "Please, call me Jan. Seeta, the boys wanted to know how GPS works. I told them that maybe you could explain it."

Mrs. Bose began to describe how GPS works.

■ ■ ■

The term *GPS* stands for "Global Positioning System." It's a worldwide **navigation** system based on radio waves. GPS was born in the late 1950s. U.S. scientists discovered that they could pinpoint the location of human-made satellites circling Earth. They could do this by studying the change in radio signals sent out by a **transmitter** on the satellite. They soon realized that this information could come in handy in

GPS uses satellite technology.

other ways. Changes in the signals received from three or more satellites could be used to determine a specific location on Earth. This idea would eventually grow into GPS as we know it today.

The world's first satellite navigation system was the U.S. Navy's Transit system. It performed well when a transmitter was at rest or moving slowly. But it did not work when the transmitter was installed on a fast-moving object, such as a fighter plane. Scientists and engineers began developing a better system. This project resulted in GPS. It took many years to develop a satellite navigation system that met the needs of the military. By the early 1990s, however, U.S. armed forces were using GPS. The technology was used to position troops, track aircraft and tanks, and locate targets. The U.S. government decided to develop GPS for civilian use.

Today, GPS is made up of three main parts: satellites, ground stations, and GPS units. A group of 24 special satellites constantly circle Earth. They send out radio signals. Six ground stations monitor the satellites. The ground stations are located in Colorado, Hawaii, Florida, Kwajalein Island, the island of Diego Garcia, and Ascension Island. GPS units have **receivers** that collect the satellite signals. Each unit's microcomputer and mapping **software** use the signals to calculate the unit's location. A GPS unit must receive signals from at least four satellites to accurately calculate its position in three dimensions.

LEARNING & INNOVATION SKILLS

The U.S. Department of Defense operates and maintains GPS. Russia has a similar satellite navigation system. Other countries are developing their own satellite navigation systems for civilian use only. The European Union is developing a worldwide system known as Galileo. The European Space Agency plans to have Galileo operating by 2013.

Some experts believe that Galileo will offer an important and useful contribution to the world of satellite navigation. They claim that Galileo will be a more accurate system. Only time will tell.

GPS units have become an important part of the global economy. The units are not only used by drivers. They are used to navigate boats and planes. Trucking companies install them to keep track of all of their trucks. Farmers use them to manage their crop fields. Biologists studying certain wild animals use GPS to record their movements and migrations. Emergency crews use GPS to respond more quickly to calls for help. Hikers use GPS to determine their position along a trail. Experts use GPS to create new maps and update old ones.

Any kind of vehicle can be equipped with a GPS system.

Manufacturing GPS units has become a global business. Companies that make GPS units can build their product at a lower cost by using **components** from many countries. Touch screens built in South Korea, plastic made in China, and U.S. software are all parts of the GPS units we use. One of the key materials used in making GPS units is a metal that humans have valued for centuries: copper.

CHAPTER TWO
A VALUABLE METAL

"Copper?" Brandon asked.

"Yes," Mrs. Bose replied. "Many different types of metal are used in the parts of a GPS unit. Companies dig up copper in

Chile's Atacama Desert is rich in minerals, including copper.

places all around the world. All kinds of businesses need copper for their products. This demand makes copper mining a big business."

■ ■ ■

People first began using copper more than 10,000 years ago. They used it to make metal tools and other objects. Today, people still search for copper. It is mined in about 50 countries around the world. Chile is the world's leading copper producer. The Radomiro Tomic mine in northern Chile opened in 1998. It is located high in the Andes Mountains, about 9,843 feet (3,000 meters) above sea level. Radomiro Tomic was the first mine developed by Codelco, a copper mining company. It produces about 7.5 million pounds (3.4 million kilograms) of copper each year. About 600 people work at the mine and its processing plants.

The Radomiro Tomic mine is a large, open pit. Workers use powerful drills to separate chunks of copper **ore** from the walls and floor of the pit. Large power shovels scoop up the chunks and drop them into huge dump trucks. The trucks carry the ore out of the pit.

Copper ore contains very little copper. Less than 1 percent of a chunk of copper ore's total weight is copper. Making copper metal from the ore takes many steps. First, the ore goes through several stages of crushing. The crushing creates a fine dust. Workers then dump the ore dust into large tubs of acid. The acid removes dirt, clay, and other unwanted materials from the metals in the ore. It takes several more steps to **refine** the copper. At the Radomiro Tomic mine, the refined copper is formed into large sheets called cathodes.

Stacks of copper sheets are bundled and ready for shipping.

21ST CENTURY CONTENT

Working at copper mines and refining plants can be difficult and dangerous. Workers sometimes protest in the hope of improving conditions. They may go on strike. During a strike, people refuse to work because of a disagreement with management over working conditions or salaries. Labor strikes occur in many industries around the world. Do you think strikes are an effective way to improve economic or working conditions for workers? Why or why not?

The heavy cathodes are loaded onto trucks. Truckers carefully drive down mountain roads to the busy port city of Antofagasta. There, shipping companies load the copper sheets onto huge cargo ships. These ships carry the copper to sites around the world. Codelco's main customers are in Asia. Its copper also goes to other locations in South America, North America, and Europe. Some of the copper is shipped to a company in Germany that is owned by Codelco. The company makes copper rods, which are used to make copper electrical wire and other products.

CHAPTER THREE

MAKING THE CONNECTION

Tommy thought about the copper. "So how is copper used in the GPS machine?"

Mrs. Bose replied, "Copper is used for the wires that connect the electronic components to each other. But the most important part that's made out of copper is the

Copper wire is an important component in many different kinds of electronic devices.

antenna. Without the antenna, the GPS unit cannot receive the satellites' radio signals. Without the radio signals, the unit cannot calculate its position or provide directions."

"Wires? Antennas?" Brandon asked. "I thought copper ore was a rock that was processed into sheets."

■ ■ ■

Copper ore is a hard rock. Pure copper, however, is soft and **ductile**. That means it can be made into long, thin strands of wire. Heat and electricity pass through copper very easily. This ability to carry an electrical current makes copper a good material for use in the wiring of many electronic products. Computer manufacturers, for example, use copper in their computer chips and circuit boards. Copper is also used in the cables that connect keyboards, printers, and other devices.

Copper has lots of other uses. It is used to make telephone lines, television cables, air conditioners, and water pipes in buildings. Copper is sometimes used to make pots and pans. Most cars contain about 50 pounds (22.7 kg) of copper.

Although copper is plentiful and relatively inexpensive, people have recycled it for thousands of years. Workers in recycling plants can process pieces of pure copper to get rid of minor **impurities**. Recycled pure copper can be used just like newly mined copper.

21ST CENTURY CONTENT

One of the metals commonly mixed with copper is beryllium. This combination makes a particularly strong alloy. Beryllium can be a health hazard if it is released into the air. Some people have a serious allergic reaction to the metal. Breathing beryllium can also lead to chronic beryllium disease. This causes permanent lung damage. Most people exposed to beryllium work in mines or in processing plants that use the metal to make alloys.

Organizations such as the Beryllium Health and Safety Committee (BHSC) raise awareness about the health risks of beryllium exposure. In what other ways do you think these organizations work to prevent people from getting beryllium-related diseases?

Copper is sometimes combined with other metals to make an **alloy**. Many times, it would cost too much to separate these other metals. In these cases, the alloys containing copper are melted. The correct amount of copper or other metals is added to create bronze and other alloys. Recycling companies then sell these alloys for use in many different types of products.

In addition to electronics, copper is often used to make pipes.

CHAPTER FOUR

PUTTING IT TOGETHER

"So," Tommy said, "miners dig up copper ore in Chile and other countries. Other workers refine the ore into copper. Then the copper can be made into lots of useful things, such as electrical wires. But who uses the copper to make GPS antennas?"

Factory workers on an assembly line build electronic devices.

"And who puts the antennas into GPS units?" Brandon chimed in.

"Companies in several different countries make GPS antennas," answered Mrs. Bose. "Like many parts used in electronic devices, most GPS antennas are made in factories in Asia. These factories are based in China, Taiwan, South Korea, and other nations. They buy copper wire and other materials from companies around the world. Workers use these materials to make GPS antennas."

■ ■ ■

Asian companies usually can sell the GPS antennas that they manufacture for less money than many other companies. That's because Asian companies have lower labor costs than competitors in other countries. Many Asian factory employees work long hours for much less pay than workers in the United States or Europe. Many Asian countries do not provide employment benefits such as vacation days and health insurance. But Asian workers are still attracted to these factory jobs. They can make more money there than in most other local jobs.

To make the most common antennas found inside GPS units, workers operate special machines. These machines coil a fine strand of copper wire around a tiny base with two flat circular ends and sides shaped like a tube. The cylinder-shaped base is usually **ceramic**. It gets attached to a small metal disk known as a ground plane. The disk helps improve the antenna's ability to receive radio signals, known as reception.

Not all GPS antennas are made in Asia. Sarantel, a company based in England, specializes in making unusually small antennas. Their antennas are used in GPS units, cell phones, and other small electronic devices. Workers at Sarantel's

Garmin has its headquarters in this building in Olathe, Kansas.

factory make antennas by using a laser to attach copper onto ceramic cylinders. Sarantel's antennas are special because they provide good signal reception without needing to be attached to ground planes. Without the ground plane, it is possible to make a much smaller antenna. Smaller antennas are very attractive to companies that build GPS devices. Many of their customers want the smallest possible GPS units.

Once GPS antennas are made, they are packed in boxes. The boxes are shipped to factories that make GPS units. Some GPS units are made in North America and Europe. Most of the companies in those countries, however, **outsource** the manufacturing step to factories in Asia. Again, lower labor costs in Asia allow companies to sell their products at lower prices.

Garmin Ltd. is one of the world's largest manufacturers and sellers of GPS units. It employs more than 7,000 workers worldwide. In the 1990s, Garmin made early GPS units that were not very accurate. The U.S. military limited the accuracy of civilian GPS to roughly 300 feet (91.4 m). It did not want anyone to use GPS to guide weapons—or for any other military use.

In 2000, the government lowered its restrictions. Civilian GPS units became accurate to about 10 feet (3 m). This change created an enormous, new market for Garmin and other GPS manufacturers: car drivers.

Garmin has offices in Olathe, Kansas, and Southampton, England. The company manufactures GPS units in Olathe and Taiwan. Garmin produces GPS technology for use in automobiles, boats, and aircraft. There are also options available for hikers and campers. But Garmin isn't the only company that produces GPS units. TomTom, a company based in the Netherlands, is the leading GPS manufacturer and seller in Europe.

Factory employees work on an assembly line to build GPS units. Each worker is assigned specific tasks as the unit moves down a conveyor belt. The unit begins to take shape as

Handheld GPS units are used by many hikers.

workers attach the antenna and a liquid crystal display (LCD) screen to the unit. Once assembled, the units are loaded with special software and tested to make sure they work properly. Finished units are packed into boxes. They're ready to be shipped to stores that sell them to consumers.

LEARNING & INNOVATION SKILLS

Two engineers, Min Kao and Gary Burrell, founded Garmin in 1989. They wanted to take advantage of GPS. The technology had just been made available to the public by the U.S. government. Today, Garmin GPS units make up about half of the total GPS sales in the United States.

What makes a business successful? There are many factors. A major one is the ability to collaborate, or work together. Companies such as Garmin would not survive if its employees did not work well together to create new and improved products. Product designers, engineers, quality testers, and sales teams all contribute their skills to make a product a hit. Can you think of more members of the team who help make GPS products a reality?

CHAPTER FIVE

SHIPPING IT OUT

After Leela's party, Mrs. Allen picked up the boys. She let Tommy take a closer look at her GPS unit. He climbed into the front seat of the car. Mrs. Allen showed Tommy how to use the touch pad on the LCD screen to type in his own address—65 Orchard Street. A map popped up on the screen. It showed the route to his house. "Wow," Tommy said. "I can't wait until my dad gets one of these. Will he have to order one all the way from Taiwan?"

"No, your father won't have to order a GPS unit from Asia," Mrs. Allen said. "He can go to a store, check out all

Huge cranes load metal shipping containers onto containerships.

of the different models, and buy the one that's right for him. Companies have set up shipping networks to transport their GPS devices from Asia—or Kansas—to our local stores."

■ ■ ■

To get GPS units from their Asian factories into the hands of their customers, companies must rely on cargo ships. Many manufacturing facilities in Asia are located in or near Hong Kong. Hong Kong is one of the world's busiest shipping centers. Crates containing electronic products such as GPS units are usually loaded into large metal shipping containers. Workers use large cranes to stack the containers on the decks of enormous containerships. The largest containerships can carry more than 10,000 containers!

Containership crews pilot their vessels to ports around the world. From Asia, they make the voyage across the Pacific Ocean to ports in North America. A common destination is Long Beach, California. It is the largest cargo port on the West Coast of the United States. Some ships pass through the Panama Canal on their way to European ports. To reach India, Africa, and the Middle East, other ships sail west through the Strait of Malacca, off the coast of Malaysia.

Once a containership docks, workers use cranes to unload the containers. They load the containers onto trucks or rail-cars. Trucks and trains carry the containers to the warehouses of GPS companies. The GPS companies truck boxes of their products to other companies that sell the units. Some products go to large retail chains, such as Walmart or RadioShack. Others go to wholesalers. Wholesalers sell products at a discount to smaller retail stores.

GPS units are often shipped across long distances to reach consumers. But GPS makers still find it less expensive to build many of their products in Asian countries than in the United States. Transporting cargo by containerships is efficient. This, combined with the low wages paid to Asian factory workers, helps keep the prices of GPS units down. Lower prices make GPS units more affordable for U.S. consumers. This helps U.S. companies make a profit for their owners.

Many stores sell GPS units.

Tommy and his father will soon go to a store to buy a GPS unit. They'll be purchasing a device that has greatly improved over the past decade. The parts used in making GPS units come from all over the world. Many workers in many countries are needed to make the devices. GPS technology has changed how drivers drive, how farmers farm, and how businesses do business. GPS devices will continue to change how people live in the 21st century.

LIFE & CAREER SKILLS

In some ways, GPS technology can help save lives. During a natural disaster, working quickly is crucial. Crews know that they must make the most of their time if they want a rescue mission to be a success. Their ultimate goal is to save as many lives as possible. Bringing disaster relief to victims quickly helps make that goal a reality. Experts use GPS and other technologies to help map a disaster area and evaluate damage levels. GPS represents one useful tool that helps rescuers solve problems and overcome the challenges of bringing aid to a disaster zone.

This map shows the countries and cities mentioned in the text. They are the locations of some of the companies involved in the making and selling of GPS devices.

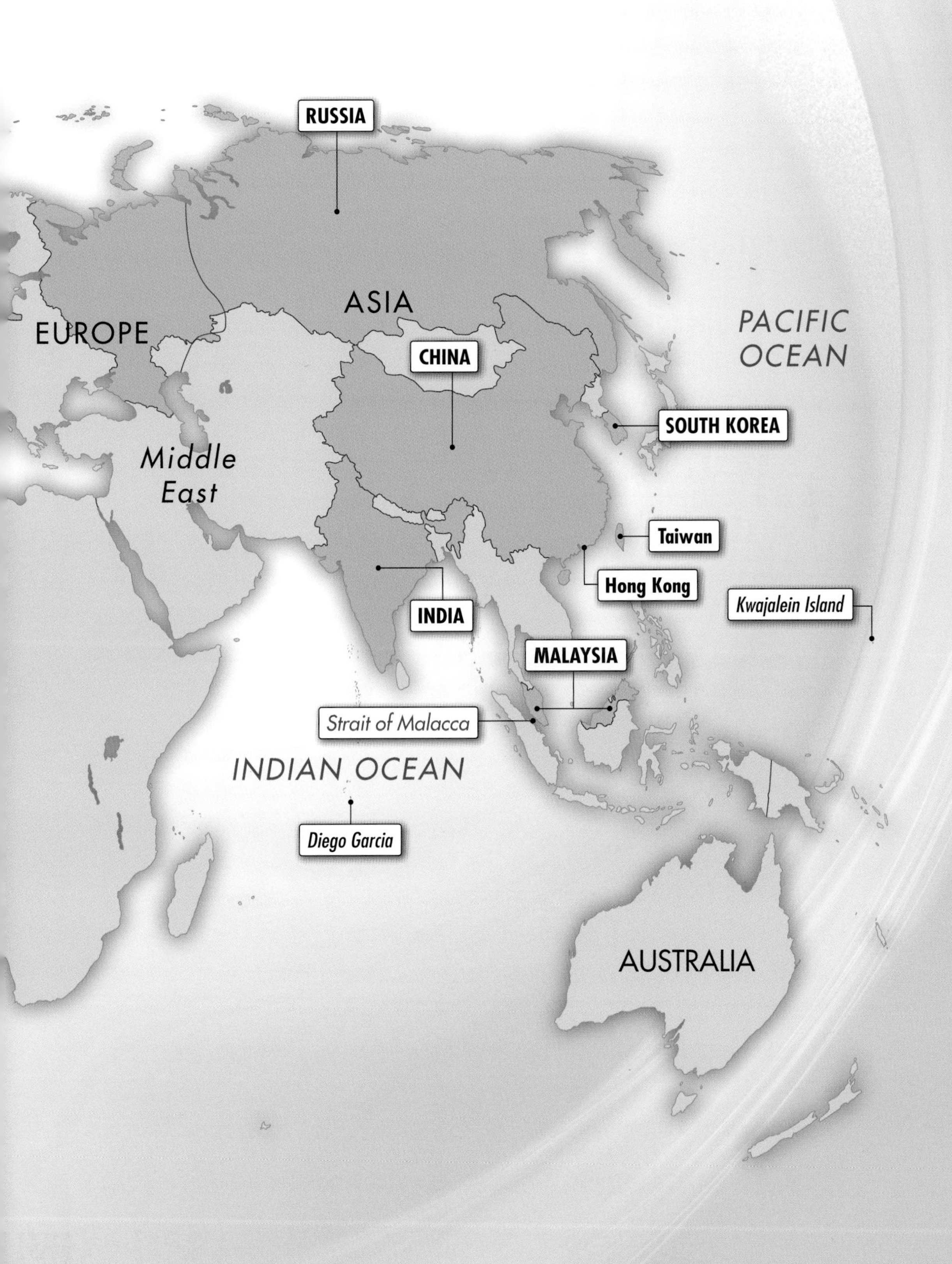
RUSSIA
ASIA
EUROPE
CHINA
PACIFIC OCEAN
SOUTH KOREA
Middle East
Taiwan
Hong Kong
Kwajalein Island
INDIA
MALAYSIA
Strait of Malacca
INDIAN OCEAN
Diego Garcia
AUSTRALIA

GLOSSARY

alloy (AL-oy) a substance made by melting and mixing two or more metals or a metal and another substance

antenna (an-TEN-uh) a device that sends or receives radio or television signals

ceramic (suh-RAM-ik) having to do with objects made of baked clay

components (kuhm-POH-nuhnts) specific pieces of a device

ductile (DUHK-tuhl) able to be stretched out into wire or hammered into thin plates

impurities (im-PYOOR-uh-teez) substances that contaminate or make something impure

navigation (nav-uh-GAY-shuhn) the science of determining the position and course of ships, aircraft, and other vehicles

ore (OR) a rock that is mined for the metal or other substances that it contains

outsource (OUT-sorss) to hire an outside company to do manufacturing or other work

receivers (ri-SEE-vurz) devices that change electrical charges or radio waves into pictures or sounds

refine (ri-FINE) to remove unwanted substances from a raw material in order to obtain a purer form of it

satellites (SAT-uh-lites) spacecraft that move in an orbit around Earth or another large body in space

software (SAWFT-wair) the programs used to run computers

transmitter (transs-MIT-ur) a device that sends out radio or television signals

FOR MORE INFORMATION

BOOKS

Flammang, James M. *Cargo Ships.* Ann Arbor, MI: Cherry Lake Publishing, 2009.

Miller, Ron. *Satellites*. Minneapolis: Twenty-First Century Books, 2008.

Sturm, Jeanne. *GPS: Global Positioning System*. Vero Beach, FL: Rourke Publishing, 2009.

WEB SITES

Copper Development Association: History of Copper
www.copper.org/education/history/copper.html
Find out more about copper's interesting history

Global Positioning System
www.gps.gov/
Explore links that describe the many uses of GPS technology

National Air and Space Museum: How Does GPS Work?
www.nasm.si.edu/gps/work.html
Learn more about how GPS satellites and receivers work

INDEX

ABOUT THE AUTHOR

G. S. Prentzas is the author of more than 20 books for young readers, including *Radar Gun* in Cherry Lake's Global Products series. He lives near New York City.